DOLLS

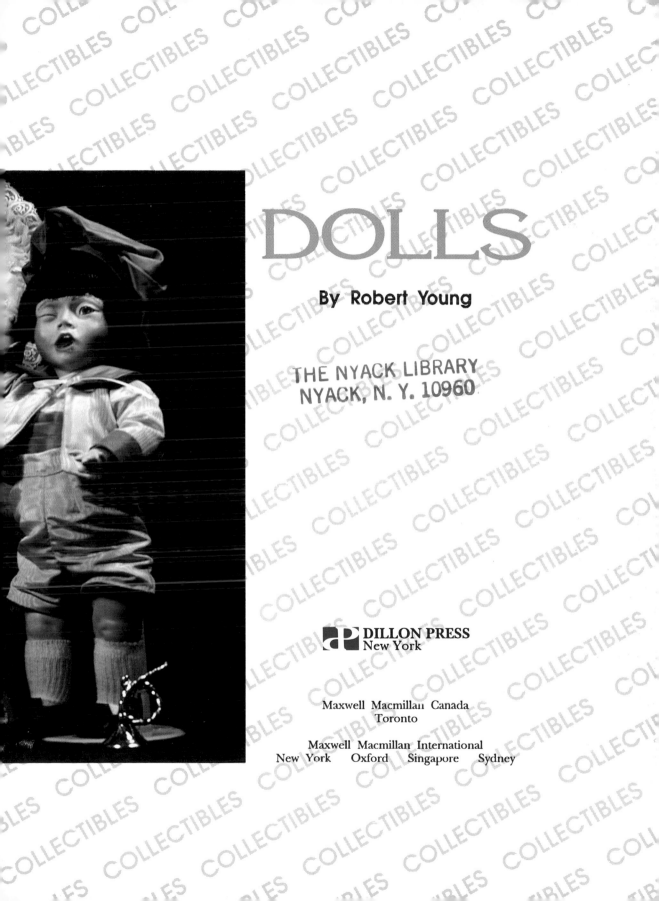

DOLLS

By Robert Young

DILLON PRESS
New York

Maxwell Macmillan Canada
Toronto

Maxwell Macmillan International
New York   Oxford   Singapore   Sydney

For Susan, who opened the door
and turned on the lights

Acknowledgments

This book would not have been written without the generous help of the following people: Shelley Andersen, Lisa Biscardi, Lara Bradley, Diane Cardinale, Linda Dalton, Leslie Dunbar, Susan Dunham, Mari Forquer, Susie Heilman, Eric Lanz, Tamara Lebovitz, Terri Lynn, Bruce McGuire, Lisa McKendall, Lloyd Middleton, Carol Murphy, Katie Nielsen, Beatrice Parsons, Jean Phifer, Tana Phifer, Terry Richardson, Steve Ryan, Donna Sanders, Edna Schora, Tom Skahill, Ken Smith, Sharon Smith, Carrie Stanoff, Joyce Stanton, David Tilbor, Shari Tsuchiyama, Valerie Williams, Jim Winkler, Susan Wissman, Sara Young, Tyler Young, Gail Zayka.

Photo Credits

Front cover images by Susan Dunham, Mattel Toys, and Doll Palace
Back cover image by Robert Young
Interior artwork by: Detroit Children's Museum, 9; Doll Palace, 58; Susan Dunham, title page, 15; Goetz Dolls, 14, 42, 47, 48, 49; Library of Congress, 25; Macmillan, Inc. 28; Mattel Toys, 6, 36; Metropolitan Museum of Art, 16; Carol Murphy, 34; Original Appalachian Artworks, 39; Robert Young, frontispiece, 10, 52; Gail Zayka, 11.

Book design by Carol Matsuyama

Library of Congress Cataloging-in-Publication Data

Young, Robert (Robert Scott). 1951-
   Dolls / by Robert Young
      p.   cm. — (Collectibles)
   Summary: Describes dolls, their history, how they are made in the present day, and how to collect and preserve them.
   ISBN 0-87518-517-7
   1. Dolls—Juvenile literature.   (1. Dolls.)   I. Title. II. Series: Collectibles
NK4893.Y68   1992   688.7'221—dc20   92-3498

Dillon Press
Macmillan Publishing Company
866 Third Avenue
New York, NY 10022

Maxwell Macmillan Canada, Inc.
1200 Eglinton Avenue East
Suite 200
Don Mills, Ontario M3C 3N1

Macmillan Publishing Company is part of the Maxwell Communication Group of Companies.

First edition

Printed in the United States of America

10 9 8 7 6 5 4 3 2 1

Some dolls, like Waldo, are based on popular characters from books.

CHAPTER 1

DOLLS, DOLLS, DOLLS

Are you looking for a new doll? If so, you're in luck. Today there are many kinds of dolls to choose from. There are dolls made in every size, shape, and color you can imagine. There are dolls big enough to hug and small enough to hide inside toy furniture. One company makes a doll that comes in a plastic cupcake. The frosting of the cupcake becomes a hat for the doll.

Dolls are figures made to look like humans. There are dolls made of people in every age group, from newborns to senior citizens. There are dolls of people from every area of the world, and dolls of famous people.

Many of today's dolls have lifelike features. Some dolls shiver. Some have hearts that beat. Other dolls can be filled with water so that they feel like real babies. There are dolls that laugh, cry, whisper, talk, and sing. You can find dolls that crawl, walk, dance, swim, and even ride a toy bicycle.

It's amazing what dolls can do. Some drink from

a bottle and wet their diapers. Others pose for you while you take their picture. Still others make a mess for you to clean up. There is even a doll that comes with a radio transmitter that makes it cry when you leave it and laugh when you come back!

Maybe you would rather have an older doll, a doll made long ago. That's no problem, either, because dolls are the world's oldest toys, and billions of them have been made for more than 2,000 years. Most have been made of materials like **china***, clay, cloth, **composition**, **papier-mâché**, wax, or wood. But dolls can be made of just about any material. Dolls have been created from apples, bones, chestnuts, coconuts, cork, corn husks, eggshells, flowers, gold, lobsters, marshmallows, metal, moss, nuts, shells, silver, soap, stones, and Styrofoam.

No matter what they have been made of, dolls have been popular. People of all ages and in all areas of the world have loved dolls throughout history, making them the most popular toys ever created.

Why have dolls been so popular? The reason is that dolls have had many uses. They have been used in religious ceremonies down through the ages. In some cultures, they have been buried with the dead. Or they have been used to put curses on enemies.

*Words in **bold type** are explained in the glossary at the end of this book.

Dolls can be made of almost any material—this one is made from a lobster shell.

A kachina doll made by the Hopi Indians. It represents the spirit of one of the tribe's ancestors.

The Hopi Indians of the southwestern United States make colorful kachina dolls, which represent the ancient spirits of the tribe. The Hopi use them to teach their children the tribe's history.

Dolls have been used to teach other things as well. Many cultures have used dolls to show girls how to care for babies. In China, dolls have been used to teach children about the correct styles

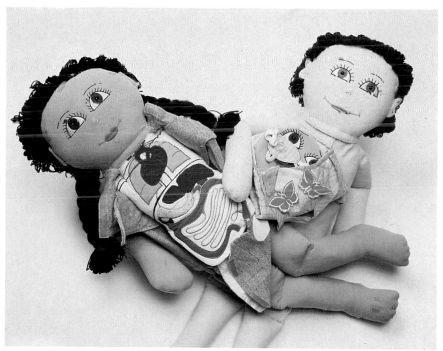

Zaadi dolls. They help kids learn about parts of their bodies.

of clothing to wear. In Japan, dolls have been used to teach children to love their country. In the United States, special dolls have been made to help children learn about their bodies and about people with handicaps.

Dolls have been important friends for children over the years. Dolls have also been great toys. They allow children to create a world of make-believe and to practice doing grown-up things. These activities are important in helping children grow and develop.

Children aren't the only people who like dolls. Adults love dolls, too. For some adults, dolls remind them of a time when they were young. For others, buying and selling dolls is a very good way to make money.

Today, dolls continue to be popular. People buy dolls as well as clothes and other **accessories** to go with their dolls. In the United States alone, people spend nearly $2 billion a year buying these things, making dolls one of the most important products in the toy industry.

The interest people have in dolls today is hard to miss. Dolls are everywhere. It isn't difficult at all to find a place to buy a new doll. Many kinds of stores sell them: department stores, toy stores, gift stores, and collectors' stores. There are doll stores that look like hospitals. Buying a doll in one of these stores is an experience like adopting a baby. You even get a birth certificate with your doll!

Some doll hospitals offer another important service. If your doll needs fixing, you can take it there. A doll doctor, someone trained and experienced in doll repair, will make your doll as good as new.

Dolls are shown in museums throughout the world. There are special doll museums, and there is even one museum that shows only one kind of doll. The Barbie Hall of Fame in Palo Alto, California, is a 16,000-piece collection of Barbie dolls and accessories. The museum was started in 1984 by Evelyn Burkhalter. It is the largest public collection of Barbies in the world.

Thousands of people collect dolls, too. And not just Barbies. All kinds of dolls are collected: baby dolls, fashion dolls, miniature dolls, handmade dolls, dolls of different countries.

The great interest in collecting dolls has brought about changes. Some collectors want high-quality dolls, so there are many doll artists hand-making dolls today. Collectors want to know about dolls, so there are many books and magazines written on the

These lifelike dolls represent children of the Akha tribe in Asia.

subject. In addition, there are clubs, doll shows, and conventions for people interested in dolls.

How did this happen? How did dolls become the most popular toy in history? It all started a long, long time ago.

- The Japanese honor their dolls at a special festival. The Festival of Dolls is held on the third day of the third month of each year.

- The most popular eye color for dolls in English-speaking countries is blue.

- One of every ten dollars spent on toys is used to buy dolls.

- 90 percent of girls between the ages of three and eleven have at least one Barbie doll.

- Animal figures are considered to be dolls by some people. The most popular animal doll has been My Little Pony. More than 160 million have been sold in more than 46 countries since 1982. One eight-year-old girl has 364 in her collection.

- Goetz makes a doll of the Akha tribe, a small group of Asian people. Part of the profits from the sale of these dolls is donated to help the Akha and other Asian ethnic groups.

This wooden paddle doll was buried with an Egyptian nobleman some 4,000 years ago. It represents his wife and was placed beside him in his tomb. That way, it was thought, they could never be parted.

CHAPTER 2

EARLY DOLLS

You may think of dolls as something to play with, but dolls haven't always been toys. The earliest dolls were not playthings at all. During the Stone Age, simple wooden dolls were made to represent gods the people worshiped. In 2300 B.C., Native Americans in Ecuador used clay dolls in their religious ceremonies.

In ancient Egypt, wooden dolls that looked like paddles were buried beside noblemen. The dolls represented their wives who, they believed, would be with them forever. Other dolls made of clay and wax were buried with people who owned slaves. The dolls were symbols of the slaves, who were believed to travel with their masters to the afterlife in order to continue serving them. Using dolls replaced an earlier custom of burying the slaves alive with their dead masters.

Children in India were once thrown into rivers when people believed the river god was angry. This practice was changed by using dolls instead of children. In China, children were not allowed to play with dolls because dolls were thought to have magical powers. In Africa, people believed dolls had evil powers and were too dangerous for children.

Over time, dolls became less important in religion, and children were allowed to play with them. Egyptian children were among the first to use dolls as toys. Their dolls were made of pottery and wood.

In ancient Greece, dolls were **mass-produced** and used for trade. They were made of **fired** clay, and some even had moving parts. The arms and legs were connected to the body with a string or cord. These were the first jointed dolls.

Greek girls played with their dolls until they married, which was at the age of 12 or 13. The girls left their dolls at the shrine of a goddess whom they worshiped. People believed that the goddess would then protect the girls.

During Roman times, children played with dolls made of clay, wood, ivory, and rags. Like the Greeks, Roman girls gave their dolls to the gods when it was time to be married.

As time passed, Europe became important in the development of dolls. With its many forests, it is no wonder that wooden dolls were popular there. Wooden dolls were made by families of craftsmen, whose skills were passed from father to son. The earlier wooden dolls were crude figures carved from blocks of wood. Most children played with these simple dolls.

Dolls for children of the rich were not so simple. These dolls wore colorful clothing, had wooden heads, and their bodies were made of leather bags filled with bran or sawdust.

Crèche dolls became popular in Europe in the early 13th century. Crèche dolls were carved figures of the Nativity scene, the birth of Christ. These figures included Jesus, Mary, Joseph, the wise men, shepherds, angels, animals, and townspeople.

Crèche dolls were displayed in many Christian homes throughout Europe during the Christmas season. They were used to educate the people about Christianity. In those days, few people could read or write. Special efforts were made to dress these dolls, and some people spent all year making clothing.

Wood wasn't the only material used to make dolls in the 1300s. Wax, papier-mâché, and composition were also used. Wax dolls were made by pouring hot wax into molds made of wood or metal. When the wax cooled, the dolls were removed and facial features were painted on. Hair was added by

This 18th-century doll was part of a crèche, or nativity scene. Her beautiful clothes took a long time to make.

using a needle to press yarn or human hair into the wax, which had been made soft by heating it.

Papier-mâché was another material used to make dolls. Papier-mâché is made by mixing plaster, glue, and paper together, putting the mixture into a mold, and then heating it.

A similar process was used to make composition dolls. The difference was in the materials used. Composition was made of glue, bran, plaster, and sawdust. Using organic materials such as bran and sawdust made these dolls popular with hungry insects.

Most of the early dolls made of wax, papier-mâché, and composition used these materials only for the parts of the dolls that didn't have clothing covering them. The parts that were covered were made of cheaper materials, such as stuffed fabric.

The end of the 1300s brought with it a new role for dolls: that of fashion models. Fashion dolls began big. The first ones were life-size, made to the exact measurements of European queens. That way, clothes could be made in one part of Europe and sent to a queen in another part.

Later, fashion dolls were made smaller and were used as an early form of advertising. Paris was the world leader in clothing fashions. But there were no fashion magazines or daily newspapers in which to show the latest styles. So designers dressed fashion dolls in small versions of their newest outfits and sent them to other cities. Designers used these dolls to show the latest in dresses, hats, shoes, and even underwear! With the help of fashion dolls, people in Europe kept in style.

Over the next several hundred years the materials and methods for making dolls improved. By the 1700s glass was being used for eyes. Glass eyes were made to open and shut by the use of a wire frame with a lead weight that hung down the inside of the doll's head.

Dolls from the 1700s show the growing interest people had in machinery. There were a variety of mechanical dolls, which had machines in them that made the dolls do many different things. The earliest mechanical dolls include ones that speak, dance, and play instruments. There was even a duck made around 1740 that quacked, ate corn, and went to the bathroom.

In the 1800s, machines helped change the doll industry in some areas of the world. As new machines were invented, they were used in making many different products, including dolls. By using machines, dolls could be made more quickly and cheaply. This made it possible for more people to afford dolls.

Wood, wax, papier-mâché, and composition dolls were still being made, but **porcelain** became important during the 1800s. Porcelain is a general term for certain types of clay that have been baked. China is porcelain that has a shiny covering, called **glaze**, put on it; **bisque** is porcelain without the glaze.

Many people like dolls made of porcelain because they look lifelike and are easy to clean. But there are problems with porcelain, too. Dolls made of porcelain break very easily.

More mechanical dolls were invented in the 1800s. Some could stand up by themselves. Some could dance the polka. One doll could even play a toy piano.

A famous walking doll was invented in the United States in 1862 by Joseph Lyon. Lyon's doll had a head made of china, leather arms, and metal feet. Her cardboard body held the small machine that made her move when it was wound with a key.

Another interesting invention came in 1889. It was a talking doll with a bisque head and a tin body. This doll was created by Thomas Edison, who also invented the light bulb and the phonograph, or record player.

Edison's talking doll had a tiny phonograph inside it that played wax records with nursery rhymes or songs on them. The dolls sold for between $20 and $25, an amount more than most people could afford in those days.

In the late 1800s, dolls began to look more like children. This was a major change because, up until then, most dolls were made to look like adults. The reason for that is simple: Being a child was not considered something special. Children were thought of as little adults, and they were expected to grow up quickly. They were dressed in the same types of clothes adults wore, and they were expected to behave like adults, including going to work.

The use of machines helped make life easier for many people, and it provided some leisure time for play and fun. Children were not needed quite as much for work, and adults began to change their views of children. These views were further changed in the early 1900s with the help of psychologists scientists who study human behavior. Psychologists said that play was good for children.

All dressed up for a tea party around the turn of the century

DOLLS

It helps them grow and develop.

New views of children helped bring about many changes in family life. They also helped bring about modern dolls.

- Some early dolls used a child's real hair for the hair of the doll.

- Paper dolls were invented in England in 1790. They were used to show the fashions of the day.

- The first American patent for a doll's head was recorded in 1858 by Ludwig Greiner of Philadelphia. The doll's head was made of papier-mâché.

- Joseph Lyon's doll was named Autoperipatekos, a Greek-based word that means "self-walking."

- During the Civil War, messages and medicines were hidden in dolls and taken across enemy lines.

- It took Thomas Edison 11 years and 14 patents before his talking doll was ready to be sold.

- Papier-mâché is a French word that means "chewed paper."

An early Raggedy Ann—the most popular cloth doll in history

CHAPTER 3

MODERN DOLLS

Modern dolls came about because of new attitudes and knowledge about children. Play was seen as important to their development. For doll makers, this was good news. Many new dolls followed.

One of the first successful American dolls was made in 1909. Its name was Billiken, and it had a composition head and a cloth body. More than 200,000 were sold at one dollar apiece in the six months after it was introduced.

The Kewpie doll, a Cupidlike figure, was created in 1912 by Rose O'Neill. She modeled it after a cute character she drew for the *Ladies Home Journal*. The doll was chubby and had a smiling face, large eyes, and a knot of hair on the top of its head, like a child who has just awakened.

Kewpie dolls have been very popular over the years. They have been made in all different sizes and from many different materials. Millions have been sold in stores and given away as prizes at amusement parks and carnivals.

Raggedy Ann is another doll that was inspired

by a drawn character. Johnny Gruelle was a newspaper cartoonist who used all kinds of dolls in his drawings. One was a rag doll based on an old, worn rag doll Gruelle had found in his mother's attic and given to his daughter, Marcella. Watching Marcella play with the doll gave him ideas for stories. It also gave him an idea for a great toy.

In 1915 Gruelle took out a patent for his doll, which he called Raggedy Ann. Then he and his family began to hand-make the dolls and sell them.

During this time Marcella, who was now 13, became very sick. Gruelle spent hours sitting by Marcella's bed, telling her stories about Raggedy Ann. After a few months, Marcella died.

Gruelle wrote down the stories he had told his dying daughter as a way of remembering her. In 1918 the first of those stories was published.

Readers loved the Raggedy Ann stories as well as the handmade dolls. It wasn't long before the demand for the dolls became so great that they had to be mass-produced in factories. Raggedy Ann was on her way to becoming the most popular cloth doll in history.

World War I brought new changes to the doll industry. Up until then, Germany had been the world leader in doll making. But, because Americans were fighting against Germany, German products were no longer welcomed in America. To keep up with the demand, more dolls had to be made in the United States.

That was fine with such companies as the Schoenhut Doll Company of Philadelphia. It had been making dolls since 1911 and had created dolls that used metal springs for joints instead of string or rubber cords.

Interest in dolls did not decrease during the war. If anything, it increased, because more dolls were being made in the United States. In the 1920s, the great interest in dolls led to the beginning of doll collecting as a hobby. With collectors came the rise of doll artists, whose handmade dolls were appreciated by collectors.

At this time, many dolls were modeled after children, but few looked like babies. That changed in 1922, thanks to the hard work of Grace Storey Putnam, a **sculptor**.

Putnam wanted to make a doll that looked like a real baby. To do that she watched babies, made notes about them, and drew them. Then she searched for a baby who could be the model for her doll's head. The model would have to be just right. Putnam wanted to find a baby who had a "fat, broad and squashed little face."

It wasn't easy for Putnam to find the right model. She went to hospitals and looked at hundreds of newborn babies. Finally she found the one she wanted. It was a three-day-old whose face was just what she was looking for.

Putnam made a wax likeness of the baby's head, then a mold from the model. When the doll was first manufactured, it had a bisque head, glass eyes, cloth body, and a crying voice. The Bye-Lo Baby looked so lifelike that it took the part of a real baby in a 1925 movie called *New Toys*.

Sales of the Bye-Lo Baby were good. They were so good that other doll companies started making their own versions of the baby doll. Fleischaker & Baum made a little girl doll named Patsy. Not only did the company sell Patsy, but it also sold a variety of clothes for Patsy to wear. This started other doll companies making clothes that were sold separately. With these clothes, called accessories, a whole new part of the doll industry was born.

It didn't take long for the idea of accessories to spread. Soon many other kinds of doll accessories were available, including bassinets, buggies, roller skates, toys, and trunks.

Another idea that spread quickly was the drink-wet doll. In 1934, Effanbee created the Dy-Dee doll. It was a baby doll that kids could really take care of. It drank from a bottle and wet its diapers. Since the doll was made of rubber, it could even be given a bath.

The Great Depression in the 1930s was a difficult time in the United States. Many people were out of work, and money was hard to come by. People were looking for something to do. They wanted a way to spend their days, and they wanted to feel good during these sad times. For many people, the movies were an answer.

Each week, 85 million people went to the movies. There they found the escape they needed from the struggles they were facing. They also found new and exciting movie stars, such as six-year-old Shirley Temple.

The Ideal Novelty and Toy Company saw a great opportunity and created the Shirley Temple doll. Ideal's designers worked hard to make the doll look just right. It took 28 models of Shirley's face before the designers were satisfied. They made the eye color hazel, just like Shirley's.

Shirley Temple, the most successful character doll ever made

The Shirley Temple doll was a great success. After each new movie, Ideal came out with a new doll dressed in the outfit Shirley had worn in that movie.

The Shirley Temple doll became the most popular **character doll** in history.

World War II helped end the Great Depression as well as bring more changes to the doll industry. The most important change was in the materials used to make dolls.

When the war started, rubber was being used to make many dolls. The rubber came from trees in different parts of the world. But wartime needs prevented some materials, including rubber, from being shipped to the United States. The shortage of rubber got scientists thinking about ways to make rubber artificially.

The results of their efforts were plastic, **synthotic** rubber, and **vinyl**. These new materials improved dolls. They made dolls feel soft and look realistic. They were washable and long-lasting. Many more dolls were made using the new materials. Some of them have been very successful.

In the 1950s, Ruth Handler enjoyed watching Barbara, her daughter, play with paper dolls. The dolls were modeled after teenagers, and the dolls had lots of clothes from which to choose. Handler, who owned Mattel Toys along with her husband, had an idea for a new doll. She decided to make a doll that looked like a teenager and wore stylish clothes.

In 1959 the Barbie doll was introduced. It cost $3, was made of hard plastic, and had movable arms and legs. Barbie came dressed in a bathing suit, sunglasses, pearl earrings, and high-heeled shoes. In addition to the doll, hundreds of clothes and accessories were made that could be bought separately.

Barbie was so popular that it wasn't long before she had friends. Her boyfriend, Ken, named after the Handlers' son, was created in 1961. Then came her best friend, Midge, in 1963; her little sister, Skipper, in 1964; Tutti and Todd, her twin brother and sister, in 1966; and Christie, her first black friend, in 1968.

At first Barbie was dressed like a fashion model. But over the years, Barbie has been dressed for many other careers, including business executive, rock star, astronaut, aerobics teacher, and surgeon. Many people think it has been helpful for girls to see Barbie in so many different roles. It tells girls that they don't need to feel limited in their choice of jobs.

Not everyone thinks that Barbie has been good for girls. Some people think that she encourages girls to be too concerned about having new and stylish

The original Barbie doll, 1959

clothes. Other people think girls will grow up wanting to look like Barbie. Having a figure like Barbie's would be impossible for most young women and very difficult for some. The result, these critics say, is that Barbie makes young girls unhappy about the way they look.

There may be disagreements about Barbie, but one thing cannot be argued: her popularity. More than 600 million Barbie dolls have been sold in 67 countries since 1959. Barbie dolls are the most popular fashion dolls in history; today one is being sold every two seconds. In addition to the dolls, you can choose from a wardrobe that grows by about 100 new outfits each year.

Barbie dolls are not the only modern success story. Another famous doll started with an idea by a 21-year-old art student. In 1977, Xavier Roberts made a doll that combined two of his interests: sculpture and quilting. He called his cloth baby dolls Little People.

But Roberts had more than a new doll. He had a new concept. The concept was to have fun by treating the dolls like real babies. So instead of making his dolls for "sale," he made them available for "adoption."

Many of Roberts's dolls were "adopted" at craft shows. Soon the demand for the dolls became so great that he and some friends rented an old medical clinic in Cleveland, Georgia, and made it into the Babyland General Hospital. Outside the hospital they planted a cabbage patch and told people that was where their doll babies came from. Each doll came with a birth certificate and adoption papers.

The hand-stitched dolls became so popular that Roberts decided to have a smaller version mass-produced. These dolls had vinyl heads and soft, pillowlike bodies. To help protect his invention, Roberts changed the name to one that could be registered and protected by law. He called his dolls Cabbage Patch Kids.

In 1983, the first mass-produced Cabbage Patch Kids hit the market. More than 3 million were "adopted" that year, making the Cabbage Patch Kids the most successful new doll ever. Since then, more than 65 million of the dolls have found homes.

The success of dolls like Barbie and the Cabbage Patch Kids helped bring about many more kinds of dolls. Today thousands of varieties are made by hundreds of doll artists, as well as by

Babyland General Hospital, home of the Cabbage Patch Kids

companies such as Applause, Corolle, Effanbee, Galoob, Goetz, Hasbro, Jesco, Kenner, Madame Alexander, PlaySkool, Reeves, Tonka, Tyco, and Victoria Impex. Today, there is a doll for everyone.

- Schoenhut dolls, which came out in 1911, were the first mass-marketed dolls in the United States.

- The name Raggedy Ann came from the titles of two poems by James Whitcomb Riley: "The Raggedy Man" and "Little Orphant Annie."

- The Bye-Lo Baby was called the "Million Dollar Baby" because it was so popular.

- Goetz began making dolls in 1950. Its first dolls were made of papier-mâché and felt, and they were stuffed with reindeer hair.

- Since 1959, more than 850 million fashions have been made for Barbie and her friends.

- The most popular Barbie fashion has been the bridal gown. Since 1959 more than 5 million have been sold.

- From 1989 to 1990 the sale of dolls in the United States grew by 20 percent.

- Every year 5,000 to 6,000 toys are introduced in the United States. Only 5 percent of the new toys will still be sold by the end of the year.

One of the first steps in making a doll: sculpting the head out of clay

CHAPTER 4

MAKING DOLLS

More than 50 million dolls are made every year. Some are hand-made by hobbyists and doll artists. Most dolls, though, are mass-produced in factories by doll companies.

Like handmade dolls, mass-produced dolls begin as ideas. Some ideas come from people who work at doll companies. Someone in the sales department might think of a doll that will sell well. An engineer might have an idea for a doll that will move in a new way. A designer might have an idea for a doll that has a different look from other dolls.

Not all ideas come from within the companies. Doll manufacturers receive new ideas from many different people. Ideas come from doll inventors, doll artists, collectors, and, of course, kids.

Doll companies differ in how they judge new ideas. In some companies, new ideas are first considered by the people in the product-development department. If an idea seems good, it will be discussed with other important people. Engineers will determine how much it will cost to produce the doll.

DOLLS

People in the sales department will figure out what the selling price of the doll should be. Then they will estimate how many dolls will be sold at that price. If it appears that the company will be able to make the profit it desires, the decision will be made to produce and sell the new doll.

Before production can begin, people in the product-development department make a plan for the doll. They make a list of all the steps that will be necessary to produce the doll. Then they make a schedule of when each step will take place.

After the plan, a product-specification (spec) sheet is filled out. The spec sheet includes important information about the doll: its size, shape, color, what it is supposed to look like, and what it is supposed to do. The spec sheet also tells what type of material the doll will be made of. The doll that will be described here will be made of soft vinyl with a body, or trunk, of stuffed fabric.

The spec sheet is sent to the design department. Using the information from the spec sheet, a designer draws a picture of the doll. When the picture matches the information on the spec sheet, the picture is sent to a sculptor.

A sculptor is an artist who makes models out of

clay, metal, plastic, stone, wax, or wood. Using tools made of wood and metal, the sculptor first makes clay models of some of the parts of the doll—its head, arms, and legs.

After the models of the doll parts have been approved, rubber molds are made. To do this, the parts are put into containers and a special liquid is poured around them. After a short time, the liquid hardens into a rubbery substance. These rubber molds are sliced open and the clay models are carefully slipped out.

Hot liquid wax is poured into the rubber molds in order to make wax models. After the wax has dried and hardened, the models are removed and inspected. The models are refined by sanding them or rubbing them with a cloth soaked in chemicals. When the models are perfect, it is time to make permanent molds.

Permanent molds are made at molding companies. The wax model parts are coated with powder made of silver, which makes it possible for electricity to pass through them. **Electrodes** are attached to the parts and then they are put into tanks. A chemical solution is poured into the tanks and strips of copper are hung in the solution. When an electric current from the electrodes is passed through the solution, tiny pieces of the copper strips move through the solution and coat the parts. Over time, the strips of copper get smaller and the coating gets thicker. It takes from eight to ten days before the coating has become thick and hard enough for the parts to be used as permanent molds. During this time, the wax has been washed out of the molds.

More models are made using the new molds. The parts are checked again and again. When they are just right, more molds are made. These are called production molds and are used in the factories to make the main parts of the dolls.

When the production molds are sent to the factory, the dolls can be mass-produced. Production molds are attached to large machines. Through small holes, workers pour the thick, liquid vinyl into the molds. Machines carry the molds into ovens that heat the vinyl to about 575°F. As the molds are heated, the machines spin them in two directions at the same time. This is done so that the vinyl will evenly coat the inside of the mold in the shape of the doll parts.

After about ten minutes of heating and spinning, the vinyl has been evenly spread and is starting to set, or become firm. The machines take the molds

Injecting liquid vinyl into the production molds

out of the ovens and dunk them in water to cool them. When the temperature is just right—about 158°F—workers use pliers and carefully pull the vinyl parts out of the molds.

The parts are inspected, separated, and put on large trays. Left arms are put on one tray, right arms on another, legs on still others. The heads, the most important parts of the dolls, are sent to be decorated.

The dolls' cheeks are sprayed with a small amount of red paint. So are other areas of the face that need a reddish highlight. Using **stencils**, workers spray on other parts of the face, such as the lips, eyebrows and, sometimes, the eyes.

Dolls that are to have plastic eyes are taken to the eye machines. These special machines first heat

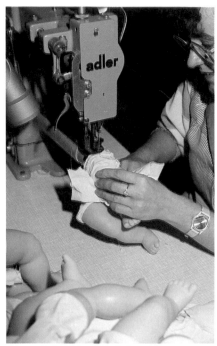

A special machine roots hair into the doll's head.

Assembling the doll: legs, arms, and head are sewn to the body.

the doll faces. Then they use thousands of pounds of pressure to force the plastic eyes into the sockets.

When the face is done, it's time for the hair to be put on. If the dolls are to have wigs, they are carefully glued on. If the dolls are to have rooted hair, the hair is attached using special sewing machines that have spools of hair rather than thread. The hair, which is sometimes real, is actually sewn into the heads.

The dolls are now ready to be assembled, or put together. Arms, legs, and heads are sewn to the fabric bodies, which have been hand-stuffed.

Completed dolls must be groomed before they

are ready to be dressed. To do this, workers use brushes with metal bristles to comb out any knots in the dolls' hair. The hair is then styled, and bows or ribbons are added.

After the dolls have been groomed, they are dressed. The clothes for the dolls have been cut out and sewn in another part of the factory while the

Dressing the finished doll

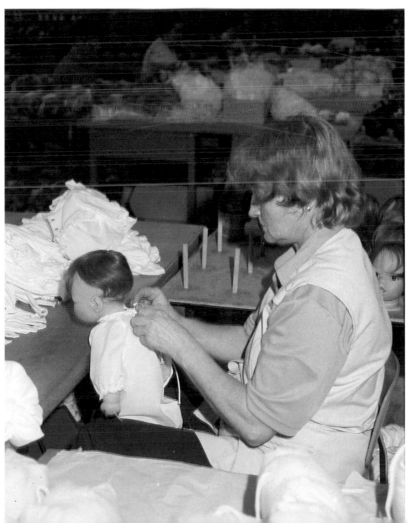

dolls have been put together. Hang tags are put on the dressed dolls. These are small pieces of cardboard with information on them: the name of the doll, the company name, the year, and any instructions for taking care of the doll.

Now the dolls are ready for their final inspection. Each doll is carefully checked. Do the clothes fit right? Are the bangs of the hair too long or uneven? Do the eyes open and close the way they are supposed to? Has the doll been painted correctly?

If the inspectors find anything wrong with a doll, they send it to be fixed. Dolls that pass inspection are packaged and then put into boxes. The boxes are shipped to every part of the world, put into all kinds of stores, and sold to all kinds of people.

- Vinyl used to make dolls is made from salt, natural gas, coal, and limestone.

- More than 90 percent of dolls are made outside the United States.

- In China, where many dolls are made, workers earn about $1.00 a day.

- More fashion dolls are made than any other kind of doll.

- There are at least 15 female dolls made for every male doll made.

- Mattel has gone through 75 million yards of fabric over the past 31 years, making it the fourth biggest maker of women's clothes in the United States.

Taking good care of your dolls is part of the fun of owning them.

CHAPTER 5

COLLECTING DOLLS

Now that you know about dolls, how would you like to start collecting them? There are many, many ways to collect dolls. Choose a way that is fun and easy for you.

To plan your collection of dolls, ask yourself some questions. First, what are you going to do with the dolls in your collection? Are you going to play with them? Are you going to display them? How long do you want to keep them? Do you want to have dolls that will be worth more as years go by?

Decide on the kinds of dolls you want in your collection. You can collect dolls of a certain size, material, or age. You can collect character dolls, dolls from different countries, or dolls all made by the same company or artist. Your collection may be made up of several kinds of dolls.

Money is also an important question. Collections can be worth anywhere from a few dollars to hundreds of thousands of dollars. How much money do you want to spend on your dolls?

DOLLS

After you decide what kind of collection you want and can afford, it's time to add to your collection. If you are interested in older dolls or dolls made by artists, it is especially important to learn about the dolls before you buy any. Read as much as you can. There are doll books and magazines as well as guides that list prices for dolls. See if your local library carries any. If not, check doll, hobby, or book stores. By reading about the kinds of dolls you want, you will learn how to identify them as well as how much they are worth.

There are other ways to learn about dolls, too. You can join doll clubs, visit museums, and talk to other collectors. Go to places where dolls are being sold, such as stores, auctions, flea markets, garage sales. Attend doll shows and conventions. Talk to people and ask lots of questions.

If you are looking for older dolls to add to your collection, talk to your relatives. Possibly some of them have childhood dolls stored away. They might even let you make their dolls part of your collection. Many people are very happy to know something they value is being appreciated and well taken care of.

You may be lucky and get dolls as gifts, but you will also buy dolls for your collection. You can find dolls for sale in many places. In addition to a variety of stores, dolls are sold at garage sales, estate sales, flea markets, auctions, and doll shows. Some dolls are sold through ads in newspapers or magazines.

When you find a doll you would like to add to your collection, think about your plan. Does the doll fit into your collection plan? Can you afford to buy it?

In buying a doll, use all the knowledge you've gained by reading and talking to people. Make sure the doll is made of what the seller says it's made of. If it's an older doll, make sure it's as old as the seller says it is. To help you, photocopy pictures of the doll you want from library reference books, then compare them with the actual doll. Check price guides to make sure the price of the doll is fair.

As you build your collection, it's a good idea to keep a record. You can do this by taking pictures of your dolls and by writing information about them. Include the following information about each doll on a separate index card:

—Doll's name
—Material it's made of
—Manufacturer
—Year it was made

—Size

—Special markings on the doll

—Price paid

—Replaced parts or repairs made

Taking care of your dolls is an important part of being a collector. It is important so that your dolls will be around for a long time for you to enjoy. It will also make a difference if you ever want to sell any of your dolls: The condition of your dolls will help determine the price you get.

The best way to care for your dolls is to use common sense. If you want to play with your dolls, do so in a way that won't damage them. If your dolls get dirty, clean them. But be careful. Different dolls require different cleaning techniques.

Most modern, mass-produced dolls made of plastic or vinyl can be easily cleaned. Run some warm water into a dish, add a few drops of a mild dishwashing detergent, and stir. Use a clean cloth to dip into the mixture and then wipe off the body of the doll. Use a cotton swab to clean the ears and nose.

Bisque dolls can be cleaned using a mild soap on the head and a liquid wax on the body. Composition dolls should be dusted instead of washed. Washing a composition doll will take the paint off.

A doll's hair and clothes are also cleaned in different ways. Some hair can be shampooed; some cannot. Some clothes can be hand-washed. Others must be dry-cleaned. And then there are the clothes that cannot be cleaned at all.

Before cleaning any doll or its clothes, check with the information booklet or hang tag that came with It. The booklet should tell you exactly how to care for your doll. If there is no booklet or other instructions, ask a doll dealer or write to the company that made the doll.

Your doll might need repair. If it needs a new part, write to the company that made it and ask for a parts list. For other problems, decide whether it's something you can fix yourself. In repairing dolls, especially older dolls, avoid doing something that can't be changed. Using something like permanent glue can make it difficult to refix a doll in the future, when there may be new techniques or materials.

If you are not sure how to make a repair, it's best to get some help. There are experts in doll repair, sometimes called doll doctors, who will fix your doll for a fee. Check the Yellow Pages under "Dolls—

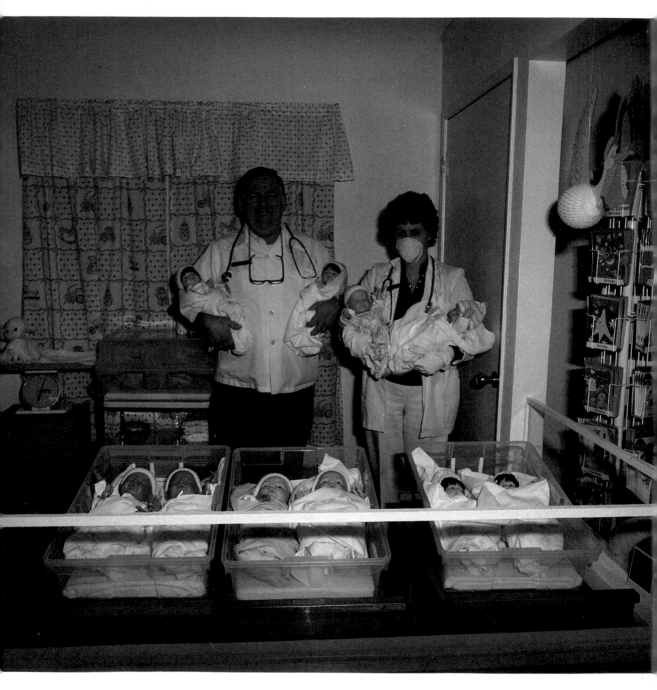

At a doll hospital you can have your doll repaired or find a "newborn" to add to your collection.

Repairing," or ask at your local doll or hobby store. Remember, though, repairing an older doll can be tricky and may result in more damage to your doll.

Most collectors like to display their dolls. This can be done in almost any way you can imagine. You can line them up on shelves, put them in cabinets, or arrange them in cases. Change your dolls' clothes to match the seasons of the year. Create scenes with your dolls: a party, a schoolroom, a favorite activity. Use stands to keep your dolls upright and accessories to add to the scenes.

At some point you might wonder how much money your collection of dolls is worth. Well, that depends. The value of each doll is based on what someone is willing to pay for it. People consider several factors when buying a doll:

—Beauty
—Identification marks
—Workmanship
—Rarity
—Condition

If you ever want to sell a doll from your collection, use your knowledge of dolls to help you set a fair price. If you're not sure what your doll is worth, get help. Some people appraise, or estimate the value of, dolls for a fee. These people are often doll dealers or people who work at auctions.

After you set a price, decide how you will sell your doll. If the doll is not worth much, a good place to sell it is at a garage sale or a flea market. If the doll is worth more than $50, place an ad in your local newspaper. You can place an ad in doll or collecting magazines, too. Or you might want to talk with other collectors or doll dealers. If you have several dolls to sell, you can rent a table at a doll show.

Collecting dolls can be an interesting and profitable hobby. Best of all, it can be fun, too. Don't forget to enjoy your dolls.

- In the United States, dolls are the second most popular item to collect. Stamps are the first.

- The largest doll club is the United Federation of Doll Clubs. It has 18,000 members.

- Keeping the original accessories as well as the box will add value to your doll.

- The most money paid for a doll at an auction was $169,576 in 1989 for a bisque doll made in 1909.

- Since fewer male dolls have been made than female dolls, **antique** male dolls usually cost more.

- A doll collector is called a "plangonologist."

DOLL TIME LINE

10,000 B.C. —Simple wooden dolls are made to represent gods.

2300 B.C. —Native Americans in Ecuador use clay dolls in religious ceremonies.

1000 B.C. —In Egypt, dolls representing slaves are buried with slave owners; Egyptian children are the first to use dolls for play.

500 B.C. —In Greece, dolls are mass-produced and used for trade.

1200s —Crèche dolls become popular in Europe.

1300s —Dolls are being made of composition, papier-mâché, wax, or wood; fashion dolls are made to display the latest clothing styles.

1700s —Many mechanical dolls are made.

1790 —Paper dolls are invented in England.

1800s —Porcelain becomes a popular doll-making material; machines become important in making dolls.

1858 —Ludwig Greiner records the first American patent for a doll's head.

1862 —Joseph Lyon makes his famous walking doll.

1889	—Thomas Edison invents a talking doll that has a tiny record player Inside it.
1909	—More than 200,000 Billiken dolls are sold in six months.
1912	—Rose O'Neill creates the Kewpie doll.
1915	—Johnny Gruelle and his family begin making Raggedy Ann dolls.
1920s	—Doll collecting becomes popular as a hobby.
1922	—Grace Storey Putnam creates the Bye-Lo Baby, a doll that looks like a real baby.
1930s	—Ideal Novelty and Toy Company produces the Shirley Temple doll.
1934	—Effanbee makes the Dy-Dee doll, a doll that drinks from a bottle and wets Its diaper.
1940s	—Synthetic rubber, plastic, and vinyl are invented and used to make dolls.
1959	—Mattel introduces the Barbie doll.
1977	—Xavier Roberts makes Little People, which will become Cabbage Patch Kids.
1978	—Gail Zayka creates the Zaadi Doll, a doll that helps kids learn about their bodies.
1989	—A 1909 bisque doll sells at auction for $169,576—the highest price ever paid for a doll.
1992	—Norwalk, Connecticut, throws a city-wide birthday celebration for Raggedy Ann.

FOR MORE INFORMATION

For more information about toys, write to:

> Communications Dept.
> Toy Manufacturers of America
> 200 Fifth Ave.
> New York, NY 10010
> (toy fact booklet "Betcha Didn't Know")

For more information about careers in toy making, write to:

> Judy Ellis, Chairperson
> Fashion Institute of Technology
> Toy Design Department
> Seventh Ave. and 27th St.
> New York, NY 10001

For more information about dolls and particular brands, write to:

> Applause, Inc.
> 6101 Variel Ave.
> P.O. Box 4183
> Woodland Hills, CA 91365

> Goetz Dolls, Inc.
> 8257 Loop Rd.—Radison
> Baldwinsville, NY 13027

Jesco, Inc.
923 S. Myrtle Ave.
Monrovia, CA 91016
(Kewpie dolls)

Original Appalachian Artworks
P.O. Box 714
Cleveland, GA 30528
(Cabbage Patch Kids)

Pleasant Company
P.O. Box 497
Middleton, WI 53562-0497
(The American Girls Collection)

Zaadi Company
836 Chelmsford St.
Lowell, MA 01851

For more information about doll magazines, write to:

Barbie Bazaar
Mural Caviale Communications
5617 6th Ave.
Kenosha, WI 53140

Barbie: The Magazine For Girls
P.O. Box 10798
Des Moines, IA 50340

Collector's Report
P.O. Box 79
Bronx, NY 10464
(newsletter for Barbie collectors)

Contemporary Doll
Scott Publications
30595 W. Eight Mile Rd.
Livonia, MI 48152

Dolls
Collector Communications Corp.
170 Fifth Ave., 12th Floor
New York, NY 10010

Doll Reader
Hobby House Press, Inc.
900 Frederick St.
Cumberland, MD 21502

Vogue Doll Club
P.O. Box 7040
San Francisco, CA 94120

For more information about doll clubs, write to:

Barbie Pink Stamp Club
Mattel, Inc.
15930 E. Valley Blvd.
Industry, CA 91744

Cabbage Patch Kids Collectors' Club
P.O. Box 714
Cleveland, GA 30528

International Rose O'Neill Club
Box 668
Branson, MO 65616

The United Federation of Doll Clubs
8 East Street
Parksville, MO 64152

Vogue Doll Club
P.O. Box 7040
San Francisco, CA 94120

Places to visit:

Barbie Hall of Fame and Doll Studio
460 Waverly St.
Palo Alto, CA 94301

The Boston Children's Museum
Museum Wharf
300 Congress St.
Boston, MA 02210

The Children's Museum
3000 North Meridian St.
Indianapolis, IN 46208

The Doll Museum of Oregon
36429 Row River Road
Cottage Grove, OR 97424

Dolly Wares Doll Museum
36th St. and Hwy. 101 North
Florence, OR 97439

Dyer-Botsford House and Doll Museum
331 First Avenue East
Dyersville, Iowa 52041
315-875-2414

Merritt Mary Doll Museum
R.D. 2
Douglassville, PA 19510

Museum of American History
Smithsonian Institute
Washington, DC 20560

The Museum of the City of New York
Fifth Avenue and 103d St.
New York, NY 10029

Strong Museum
One Manhattan Square
Rochester, NY 10467

Washington Dolls' House and Toy Museum
5236 44th St., NW
Washington, DC 20015

GLOSSARY

accessories (ak-SES-uh-reez)—items such as clothes, toys, or furniture that are used with dolls

antique doll (an-TEEK)—a doll made more than 100 years ago

bisque (BISK)—porcelain without a glaze

character doll—a doll that looks like a real person, especially a baby or child

china—porcelain with a glaze

composition (kom-pah-ZISH-un)—material used to make dolls; made of glue, bran, plaster, and sawdust

crèche doll (KRESH)—figure from a scene of the birth of Christ

electrode (e-LEK-trode)—a small device through which electricity flows

fire—to heat until hard

glaze—a smooth, shiny finish put on some porcelain

mass-produce—to make many

papier-mâché (pay-per-mah-SHAY)—material used to make dolls; made of plaster, glue, and paper

porcelain (POOR-sa-lin)—clay that has been heated until it is hard; may be glazed or unglazed

sculptor (SKULP-ter)—an artist who makes models out of clay, metal, plastic, stone, wood, or wax

stencil—a thin piece of material with parts cut out; used to paint certain parts of dolls

synthetic (sin-THET-ik)—something made artificially, using chemicals

vinyl (VINE-ul)—a type of plastic

INDEX

ABOUT THE AUTHOR

A fourth-grade teacher and free-lance writer, Robert Young is fascinated by kids and the things they collect. In addition to the books in the Collectibles series, Mr. Young has written about a wide range of subjects. *The Chewing Gum Book* and *Sneakers: The Shoes We Choose!* are two of his titles recently published under the Dillon Press imprint. Mr. Young lives with his family in Eugene, Oregon, and enjoys visiting schools and talking to teachers and students about writing.